ALFIE

BOE

A Detailed Biography

John Brooklyn

Table of Contents

In Fleetwood

Alfie had a remarkable upbringing, despite being the youngest of nine children in working-class Fleetwood, Lancashire. His heritage is a blend of Irish and Norwegian roots. Interestingly, he goes by the name Alfred Giovanni Roncalli Boe, even though he has no Italian ancestry whatsoever. His parents simply chose to give him the Italian version of Pope John XXIII's name.

Alfie received his education in Fleetwood, attending the Catholic institutions of St. Wulstans, St. Edmunds, and Cardinal Allen High School. Throughout Boe's journey, music remains deeply ingrained in their life. In fact, his passion for performing music was evident even before he was born. While Alfie's mother was pregnant, she was engrossed in a concert on television. In a moment of pure excitement, Alfie kicked within his mother's womb, causing her tea cup to soar through the air as the drummer embarked on an unexpected solo.

Listening to his father's Richard Tauber albums, where he first heard Puccini's La Bohème, is one of Alfie's earliest musical memories. His father played a significant role in shaping his upbringing, not only because of his beautiful voice but also because he often serenaded the family with his songs. They bonded over their shared love for music, spending countless hours listening to albums together.

However, tragedy struck when Alfie was just 23 years old, as his father succumbed to a brain tumour. Despite this devastating loss, Alfie found the strength to put on a concert shortly after. During this performance, he felt his father's presence and, just as he had done when his father was alive, called for his help.

Since that moment, every time Alfie prepares to step onto the stage, he quietly asks his dad, "Can you give me a hand?" He believes that his father's support will lead him to a resounding success. This heartfelt connection between father and son continues to inspire Alfie, driving him to deliver exceptional performances time and time again.

As the youngest of nine children, he would often join his mother in the kitchen, listening to Paul McCartney's "Mull of Kintyre" while she fried cod. At the tender age of three, he began nurturing his natural talent for music. Unbeknownst to him, his impromptu performances of Elvis tunes and children's songs would often leave his siblings and spouse in fits of laughter.

Boe's first taste of the spotlight came at the age of 14, when he made his public debut in a Songs from the Shows show at Fleetwood's Marine Hall. Under the guidance of the remarkable local singing instructor, Lottie Dawson, he nervously sang a few lines. Reflecting on that moment, he admitted to feeling a mixture of excitement and anxiety. While his father introduced him to the world of opera through albums, it was his brothers who exposed him to a wide range of musical genres, from Elvis to La Boheme.

Unfortunately, his school did not offer music lessons, as they required students to play instruments such as the piano or violin and he didn't want to settle for any. This restriction prevented him from pursuing his passion for music within the school's curriculum. At the age of 17, he made the bold decision to drop out of college without obtaining any A-levels. Instead, he embarked on a new journey as an apprentice at the prestigious TVR sports car plant in Blackpool.

Surprisingly, even renowned celebrities like Tom Jones and the Pet Shop Boys sought his services as a personal security guard in their dressing rooms. To the delight of his coworkers, he would serenade them with opera arias while meticulously polishing automobiles. It was during one of these moments that fate intervened. A customer with connections in the music industry overheard his enchanting voice and urged him to venture to London and audition for the esteemed DOyly Carte Opera Company.

With only one classical piece, *"You Are My Heart's Delight"* from Franz Lehár's "*The Land of Smiles,*" in his repertoire, he nervously arrived at the audition wearing a humble ensemble of a lumberjack shirt, T-shirt, jeans, and boots. As he glanced around, he couldn't help but notice the impeccably dressed individuals, resembling opera Kens and Barbies, surrounding him. Doubt crept in, making him question his place among them. However, against all odds, his audition turned out to be a success.

Two weeks later, an invitation arrived, beckoning him to join the chorus for the upcoming tour. This opportunity meant leaving behind his job as a car cleaner and embarking on a year-long singing career. Although his dream was to become a rock star, he recognized the importance of classical training in a singer's development.

Unfortunately, due to a misplaced business card, he has been unable to locate the person who initially recommended him for the audition. Nonetheless, this serendipitous encounter forever altered the course of his life, propelling him towards a future filled with musical triumphs and unexpected adventures.

In The Entertainment Industry

In London, Alfie Boe actively participated in the prestigious Vilar Young Artists Programme at the Royal Opera House, pursued his studies at the renowned Royal College of Music, and showcased his talent with the National Opera Studio. During this time, he also gained recognition as the opera sensation through his appearances with the Clint Boon Experience, a band led by the former keyboardist of the Inspiral Carpets, in their albums released in 1999 and 2000.

In 1999, Boe embarked on an extensive tour throughout Scotland, captivating audiences with his portrayal of Ernesto in Scottish Opera's Opera-Go-Round production of Don Pasquale.

After two years of searching for the perfect fit, Baz Luhrmann finally discovered Boe and cast him in the lead role of La Bohème. This collaboration led to Boe's inclusion in the 2002 Broadway Cast Recording by Bazmark Live, where he was credited as Alfred Boe. The exceptional performances of Boe and his fellow cast members were recognized with Tony Awards in 2003, solidifying their status as outstanding talents in the industry.

Boe's remarkable abilities have also been showcased by the English National Opera and Glyndebourne, both of which have featured him in prominent roles, further cementing his reputation as a sought-after performer in the opera world.

"Alfie Boe's CD, *Classic FM Presents Alfie Boe*, reached an impressive #3 on the UK classical chart. This achievement came after he signed with the label in 2006, becoming the first artist in a new initiative for the renowned radio station.

A notable performance took place on October 27, 2006, when Boe and singer Hayley Westenra mesmerized the audience at Canterbury Cathedral as part of the esteemed Canterbury Festival. Following this success, Boe inked a deal with EMI Classics in November 2006, leading to the release of his debut album, *Onward,* in March 2007.

In that same month, Boe showcased his vocal prowess alongside soprano Natasha Marsh during the inaugural Classic FM webcast concert. Prior to this, he embarked on a tour across the United Kingdom in February, sharing the stage with the Fron Male

Voice Choir. Additionally, Boe's dedication to the arts led him to become an ambassador for the Prince of Wales Arts & Kids Foundation, a prestigious British organization that harnesses the power of the arts to inspire and educate young individuals. Boe's mission as an ambassador is to introduce these youngsters to the enchanting world of opera and the boundless joys of musical expression."

In April, Boe made an appearance alongside Lesley Garrett and Willard White at the prestigious Royal Albert Hall for the ITV Music of Morse event. Adding to his achievements, on May 3, 2007, he received a nomination for the Classical BRIT Award for Best Album, although ultimately losing out to the legendary Paul McCartney.

Continuing his impressive collaborations, Boe joined forces with Michael Ball in the remarkable staging of Kismet at the esteemed English National Opera. His exceptional rendition of *"Stranger in Paradise"* from Kismet was featured on the Michael Parkinson programme. This outstanding performance was later released as a digital single, showcasing Boe's incredible talent in a live setting.

In August, Boe fulfilled a lifelong dream by releasing *"La Passione,"* an album of Neapolitan music. Showcasing his versatility, he shared the stage with the talented Natasha Marsh at the esteemed Arundel Festival on August 24, 2007. Continuing to enthrall audiences, Boe delivered a mesmerizing performance at Canterbury Cathedral during the Canterbury Festival on October 19, 2007.

In November 2007, Boe graced the iconic Royal Albert Hall once again, delivering a powerful performance for the annual Festival of Remembrance.

Boe sang at the special Music Quest event at the Pleasure Beach Arena in Blackpool on January 31, 2008. The purpose of the event was to introduce over 1,600 local children to classical music. This event marked the conclusion of the three-year Music Quest initiative, which was supported by the Prince of Wales Arts & Kids Foundation and Classic FM MusicMakers.

In 2009, Alfie had the opportunity to perform with the Scottish Opera Orchestra. He brought his unique charisma to the enchanting melodies of Léhar.

While growing up, Alfie developed a deep appreciation for Richard Tauber's work. Inspired by his father's favourite singer, Richard Tauber, he collaborated with Linn Records to record his passion project, *Franz Lehár: Love was a Dream.*

During the 20th century, the Austro-Hungarian composer Franz Lehár (1870-1948) created some of the most iconic and beautiful music in operetta. His compositions were characterized by poetic and melodious melodies and a blend of drama and romance.

From March 29 to June 12, 2016, the renowned Broadway production, *Finding Neverland,* captured the attention of the audiences with its enchanting story. In this remarkable play, the talented Boe took on the lead role of J. M. Barrie, bringing the character to life with his exceptional performance.

Continuing his streak of remarkable performances, Boe graced the stage once again in a limited run of Rodgers and Hammerstein's *Carousel* at the English National Opera. Under the brilliant direction of Lonny Price and alongside the mesmerizing mezzo-soprano Katherine Jenkins, Boe portrayed the romantic lead, Billy Bigelow. This captivating production ran from April 7 to May 13, 2017, leaving audiences in awe of Boe's incredible talent.

Carousel, a musical collaboration between Richard Rodgers and Oscar Hammerstein II, marked their second successful partnership. The story revolves around the charismatic carousel barker, Billy Bigelow, who falls deeply in love with Julie Jordan, a hardworking mill worker. However, their careers suffer as a consequence of their love affair. In a desperate attempt to support Julie and their unborn child, Billy becomes involved in a robbery, but tragically, their plan takes a disastrous turn.

Act One of the musical is set in 1873 in Maine. It begins by introducing the audience to two young female millworkers who embark on an enchanting evening at the town's carousel. Our protagonist, Julie Jordan, captures the attention of the charismatic barker, Billy Bigelow, and the two find themselves riding the carousel together, their hearts entwined. However, their budding romance is met with jealousy from Mrs. Mullin, the owner of the carousel, who forbids Julie from returning. In a fit of rage, Billy mocks Mrs. Mullin during a heated argument with

Julie and her friend, Carrie Pipperidge, resulting in his dismissal from the job.

Seeking solace, Billy invites Julie for a drink, hoping to drown his sorrows and perhaps find comfort in her presence. Meanwhile, Carrie, who is engaged to Enoch Snow, a fisherman, probes Julie about her feelings for Billy as he gathers his belongings. Despite Carrie's persistence, Julie remains tight-lipped, leaving her true emotions concealed.

When Julie declines the mill owner's offer of a ride home, she unknowingly seals her fate and loses her job. Left alone, Billy and Julie engage in a heartfelt conversation, speculating on the possibilities of love between them. However, neither of them dares to utter those three little words that could change everything.

After weeks of preparation, the highly anticipated summer clambake is finally taking shape. Julie and Billy, now married, have made their home in the spa owned by Julie's cousin, Nettie. However, their domestic bliss is shattered when Billy, burdened by his unemployment, allegedly assaults Julie, and then she confides in her friend Carrie.

Amidst the chaos, Carrie brings some much-needed joy by announcing her engagement to Enoch, who unexpectedly bumps into her conversation with Mister Snow about him. Tensions escalate when Billy and his reckless whaler companion, Jigger, make their entrance, openly displaying their contempt towards Enoch and Julie. As Billy and Jigger turn to leave, Julie becomes more perturbed. Meanwhile, Enoch confides in Carrie his ambitious dreams of starting a large family, surpassing her own expectations, and his aspirations of achieving wealth through herring sales.

In this scene, Jigger and his crewmates regale the audience with their thrilling tales of life at sea. Jigger, always the schemer, tries to convince Billy to join him in a daring heist. However, Billy, aware of the risks involved, declines the offer. Despite Mrs. Mullins' persistent efforts to lure him back to the carousel, Billy is hesitant to return considering the fact that he is married to Julie.

The news of Julie's pregnancy fills Billy with immense joy, making him more reluctant on working on the carousel again. However, he understands the importance of supporting his future family, so he reluctantly agrees to become Jigger's sidekick. As the entire town prepares for a clambake,

Billy decides to join them, knowing that his and Jigger's alibi hinges on being seen there.

The second act opens with scenes of a lively clambake, brimming with laughter and cherished memories. Amidst the festivities, Jigger attempts to seduce Carrie, but it ruins her relationship with Enoch as he bumps into them. Julie, seeking solace, finds comfort in the love of her partner, while Carrie leans on her friends for support.

As Billy and Jigger prepare to leave, Julie senses something amiss and detects the presence of a concealed knife under Billy's shirt. Desperate, she pleads with him to hand it over, but he stubbornly refuses and departs to carry out the heist.

Jigger and Billy while away the hours with a game of cards, biding their time in anticipation. Little did they know that their audacious plan to steal the mill's funds had already been thwarted. Mr. Bascombe, their intended victim, had cunningly deposited the money, leaving them empty-handed. As the realization dawns on Billy, defeat washes over him, rendering his further involvement utterly futile.

Suddenly, the atmosphere shifts dramatically. Bascombe, brandishing a revolver, confronts Billy, putting an abrupt end to their ill-fated heist. In a desperate bid to escape, Jigger flees the scene, leaving Billy to face the consequences alone. Overwhelmed by despair, Billy takes his own life, plunging a knife into his chest. It is at this very moment that Julie arrives, just in time to hear his final words.

With remarkable composure, Julie professes her love for Billy, her gentle touch soothing his troubled soul. Nettie, sensing Julie's anguish, arrives to offer her unwavering support, providing the strength she needs to persevere through the heart-wrenching ordeal. Meanwhile, Carrie and Enoch, brought together once more by this catastrophic event, join forces to console Julie, offering solace in the face of overwhelming sadness.

Billy's stubborn spirit is whisked away to meet the celestial authority known as the Starkeeper. With an air of authority, the Starkeeper informs Billy that his virtuous deeds in life were insufficient to secure him a place in paradise. However, a glimmer of hope emerges as the Starkeeper reveals that Billy may return for a single day to embark on a redemptive mission, provided there is someone on Earth who remembers him.

Fifteen long years have elapsed since Billy's tragic suicide, and the Starkeeper discloses a tantalizing proposition: he may save his daughter, Louise, and thereby earn his passage into paradise. In a mesmerizing ballet of instrumental beauty, the Starkeeper guides Billy's gaze from the heavens, allowing him to search for his estranged daughter. Alas, Louise has metamorphosed into a desolate and embittered adult, burdened by the stigma of her father's criminal past and abusive behaviour. The neighbourhood children, recoiling from the sins of her father, shun her mercilessly.

To compound her misery, a young ruffian, reminiscent of her father's own troubled youth, toys with Louise's emotions, only to abandon her cruelly at the dance. Billy, consumed by a mix of relief and concern, eagerly awaits the conclusion of the dance, yearning to return to Earth and tend to his beloved child. Seizing a fleeting opportunity while the Starkeeper is momentarily distracted, Billy cunningly absconds with a star, his determination unyielding.

Carrie recounts her exhilarating journey to the bustling city of New York alongside the now-affluent Enoch, as they find respite outside Julie's charming cottage. Suddenly, Carrie's husband and a few of their children enter the scene, urgently reminding her of the impending preparations for their high school graduation. However, their eldest son, Enoch Jr., opts to remain behind, seeking a private conversation with Louise, while Billy and his ethereal companion, the Heavenly Friend, make their timely arrival.

In this clandestine tête-à-tête, Louise confides in Enoch Jr., expressing her fervent desire to abandon her familial abode and join a vibrant theatre troupe. Enoch Jr., in a desperate attempt to dissuade her, proposes marriage as a means to prevent her departure, albeit aware of his father's disapproval. As tensions escalate, both of them hurl insults at each other's fathers, further fueling Louise's fury, and prompting her to demand Enoch Jr.'s immediate departure.

In the midst of this emotional turmoil, Billy, with his uncanny ability to materialize anywhere, approaches a distraught Louise, claiming to be a confidant of her father. As a token of his presence, he presents her with a stolen star from the heavens above. However, when Louise declines this peculiar offering, Billy's frustration manifests in a swift slap upon her hand. In a mysterious twist, he vanishes into thin air, leaving Louise to recount the bewildering encounter to Julie. She describes the slap as more of a caress than a blow, leaving Julie hanging onto every word, captivated by the unfolding events. Feeding her solitude, Louise retreats indoors while Julie's attention is caught by the fallen star belonging to Billy; sensing his presence, she holds onto it tightly.

In a final, desperate attempt to aid his daughter and seek redemption, Billy clandestinely attends Louise's graduation ceremony. Dr. Seldon, a renowned and esteemed physician in the town, imparts invaluable wisdom upon the fresh-faced graduates, cautioning them against placing excessive importance on their parents' triumphs or failures. As Seldon issues the command, a harmonious chorus of "You'll Never Walk Alone" resonates through the air, uniting the graduates in a powerful display of solidarity.

With trepidation, Louise tentatively extends her hand towards another girl, only to discover that she need not endure the torment of being an outcast any longer. This newfound acceptance is a direct result of the profound words whispered by the invisible presence of Billy, urging her to place her trust in Seldon's guidance. Finally, Billy musters the courage to confront Julie, baring his soul and expressing his deep affection for her.

In a poignant and awe-inspiring moment, Billy is carried away to his celestial reward, while his devoted wife and children serenade him with heartfelt melodies.

***

The performances of Alfie Boe and Katherine Jenkins in *Carousel* received high praise from critics. One reviewer was particularly impressed by the exceptional talent displayed by the lead vocalists, as well as the flawless execution of Rodgers' work by the 42-piece orchestra.

On October 3, 2010, in celebration of the show's 25th anniversary and the release of the accompanying DVD and Blu-ray Disc, Boe took on the role of Jean Valjean in a concert performance of Les Misérables at London's O2 Arena.

Les Misérables is set in early 19th century France and follows the story of Jean Valjean, a French peasant who is released from prison in 1815 after serving 19 years. His sentence was initially for stealing bread to feed his sister's starving child, and he later accumulated additional years for multiple escape attempts. The narrative unfolds as Valjean experiences a life-changing act of kindness from a bishop, prompting him to abandon his parole and embark on a new path. However, Inspector Javert of the police force relentlessly pursues Valjean, determined to bring him to justice. The story reaches its climax during a French revolution, where Valjean and a diverse cast of characters find themselves entangled in a battle against the government, taking refuge behind a barricade in the streets of Paris.

In December 2010, a re-recorded version of the concert encore performance of *"Bring Him Home"* was released as a charity CD single and download from Abbey Road Studios. The credit for this rendition goes to the Valjean Quartet—Boe with Colm Wilkinson, Simon Bowman, and John Owen-Jones all of whom have portrayed Valjean in various theatrical productions.

On December 16, 2010, in front of Charles, Prince of Wales, and Camilla, Duchess of Cornwall, Boe reprised his role as Valjean at the Royal Variety Performance.

Approximately eleven days after its initial announcement, Decca Records released *"Bring Him Home"* as Alfie's fifth studio album in the United Kingdom. From June 23 through November 2011, Boe played Valjean in Les Misérables at London's Queens Theatre. His close friend, Matt Lucas, also joined the cast in the role of Thenardier. In August of that year, Boe appeared at Beau Sejour and

Gloucester Hall with the National Symphony Orchestra.

Alfie's sixth studio album, aptly titled *"Alfie,"* was released three months later. This highly anticipated album marks a significant milestone in Alfie Boe's career. In October 2011, Decca Records, a renowned UK-based record label, proudly unveiled this masterpiece to the British audience. The album quickly climbed the ranks, securing an impressive position at number 6 on the prestigious UK Albums Chart.

Following the success of *"Alfie,"* the talented artist released another studio album, *"Storyteller,"* a year later. Once again, Decca Records took charge of its production This album, too, made its mark on the UK

Albums Chart, reaching an admirable position at number 6.

Continuing his fruitful collaboration with Decca Records, Alfie's following studio album for the label, *"Trust,"* was released amidst great anticipation. Despite being released in the middle of the year, *"Trust"* managed to captivate audiences and secured a respectable position at number 8 on the UK Albums Chart.

In 2016, Alfie Boe unveiled his ninth studio album, *"Serenata."* This enchanting collection of songs resonated with fans across the United Kingdom, peaking at an impressive number 14 on the chart. Notable tracks such as *"Serenata Celeste," "Volare,"* and *"Mambo Italiano"* showcased Alfie's exceptional vocal prowess and his ability to breathe new life into classic melodies. On November

17, 2014, *"Serenata"* became available for purchase as a digital download and on compact disc, further expanding its reach. The album's undeniable charm and Alfie's devoted fanbase contributed to its remarkable success, with over 60,000 copies sold in the UK, earning it a well-deserved silver certification.

In 2015, the highly anticipated staging of *Les Misérables* on Broadway at the prestigious Imperial Theatre in New York City marked a triumphant return for the talented performer, Alfie Boe, who reprised the iconic role of Valjean. This momentous occasion was particularly significant as it coincided with the departure of Ramin Karimloo, who had portrayed the character of Enjolras for an impressive 25 years.

Following this impressive milestone, Boe confirmed his reprisal of the role of Valjean in a captivating staged concert performance of Les Misérables at London's esteemed Gielgud Theatre in February 2019. Sharing the stage with the esteemed John Owen-Jones, who portrayed the character alongside him, Boe delivered a mesmerizing performance that left audiences in awe. Notably, he was joined by the immensely talented Michael Ball, with whom he had previously collaborated, in the role of Inspector Javert, as well as the versatile Matt Lucas, who portrayed Thénardier. This remarkable run of performances commenced on August 10 and concluded on December 2, captivating audiences at the renowned Gielgud Theatre in London.

Other Career Engagements

In January of 2011, Boe graced the stage of the English National Opera, fascinating the audiences with his mesmerizing performances in the renowned productions of La Bohème and The Mikado. But his musical journey didn't stop there. Boe's enchanting voice echoed through the halls of Idaho in March, where he delivered three awe-inspiring performances. Two of these remarkable shows took place in the charming town of Rexburg, while the other unfolded in the picturesque setting of Sun Valley.

April brought forth two quintessentially British events, where Boe's melodic prowess took centre stage. First, he graced Trafalgar Square with a magnificent concert honouring St. George's Day.

Shortly after, Boe enchanted audiences once again, this time at the Criterion Theatre, where he starred in the production of The Great British Musical: *The Famous and the Future.*

As the summer sun bathed the land in its golden glow, Boe continued to delight hearts and minds. On June 18, 2011, he closed the festival at the majestic Hampton Court Palace, leaving a lasting impression on all who were fortunate enough to witness his performance. Prior to this grand finale, Boe had already graced the esteemed Royal Albert Hall on the Isle of Man, headlining the prestigious Classical BRIT Awards ceremony in May.

September brought new heights of musical excellence for Boe, as he took the stage in two extraordinary concerts hosted by the esteemed BBC. The first, the Last Night of the Proms, took place at the illustrious Caird Hall, where Boe's voice soared to new heights, leaving the audience in a state of pure euphoria. Shortly after, he graced the Tabernacle Chapel in Llanelli, lending his extraordinary talent to the Grand Performance Concert hosted by the Llanelli Choral Society.

In December of 2011, "Alfie Boe 'Bring Him Home' UK Concert Tour" kicked off in Bristol, and ended in the first week of February 2012, at the Gateshead Sage.

Boe's appearance at the Lytham Proms Festival Weekend in August 2012, held in Lytham St. Annes, just a stone's throw away from his birthplace of Fleetwood, was an unforgettable experience. The local publication, *The Blackpool Gazette*, aptly titled his performance "Bring Him Home," capturing the essence of a heartfelt homecoming.

Prior to this, Boe mesmerized audiences with a performance at the Kauffman Centre in Kansas City, Missouri, in May 2012. His voice also aired the atmosphere during the celebration of Queen Elizabeth II's Diamond Jubilee in June 2012. Starting with the timeless classic *"O sole mio,"* Boe effortlessly transitioned into Elvis Presley's iconic *"It's Now or Never."* However, the pinnacle of this momentous occasion was when Boe, alongside the esteemed American singer Renee Fleming, graced the balcony of Buckingham Palace, delivering a breathtaking rendition of *"Somewhere"* from the beloved musical West Side Story. It was an unprecedented honour for someone outside the royal family to stand on that balcony.

Boe's star power continued to rise as he made a memorable appearance on The One Show in August 2012. But the real highlight was yet to come. Embarking on a grand North American concert tour, Boe kicked off the extravaganza on October 2, 2012, in Dallas, Texas. The tour concluded on October 29, 2012, in Toronto, Ontario, leaving a trail of mesmerized fans in its wake.

Boe graced the stage as a distinguished guest performer for the Mormon Tabernacle Choir, Orchestra at Temple Square, and Bells on Temple Squares 2012 Christmas performance series. The event also had highlights from the legendary broadcaster, Tom Brokaw, who lent his captivating voice to narrate the awe-inspiring tale of Gail Halvorsen and the courageous sugar bombers of

World War II. To everyone's delight, Halvorsen herself made a special appearance, adding an extra touch of authenticity to the performances. Boe, with his mesmerizing vocals, not only delivered a breathtaking rendition of *"Bring Him Home"* but also enchanted the audience with a medley of beloved holiday classics. The magic of these live performances has been immortalized in the remarkable recording, *"Home for the Holidays Featuring Alfie Boe."*

In a return to the United States, Boe embarked on a tour spanning eight vibrant cities from January 27 (starting in New York) to February 9 (concluding in Pennsylvania). Boe often hailed as the Lancashire Michael Bublé, achieved an amazing feat in February 2013 when two of his albums, *"Alfie"* (2011) and *"Bring Him Home"* (2010), were certified platinum by the prestigious BPI. He kicked off a tour in Birmingham, marking the first stop of Boe's exhilarating three-week, fourteen-city journey, culminating in a grand finale in Belfast, Northern Ireland. Recognizing his talent and contributions to the world of music, the esteemed Royal College of Music bestowed upon Boe the distinguished honour of a Fellowship in April 2013. Boe's awe-inspiring rendition of *"Bring Him Home"* resonated deeply with the hearts of the nation as he graced the stage during the 2013 U.S. National Memorial Day Concert on the majestic West Lawn of the Capitol.

In 2014, Alfie Boe brilliantly reimagined Pete Townshend's iconic Quadrophenia alongside the esteemed London Philharmonic Orchestra. Recognizing the potential of a classically trained singer's voice in this genre, Boe fearlessly embraced the challenge. Singing this music proved to be more demanding than opera itself, but he revelled in the exhilarating test it presented. Boe astutely compared the energy, optimism, and power of this musical masterpiece to the symphonies of Beethoven or Mozart. Hence, Pete Townshend's Classic Quadrophenia rightfully claimed its place as the official title of the album.

However, Boe faced ridicule from the classical music community for his audacious claim of finding opera boring and abstaining from attending performances. Undeterred by the naysayers, Boe remained steadfast in his belief, unapologetically forging his own path in the industry.

In a remarkable display of versatility, Boe stepped in for the indisposed Colm Wilkinson to conduct the esteemed Phoenix Symphony for two extraordinary performances on June 4 and 5, 2015, at the renowned Symphony Hall.

In the Last Decade

In an episode of the British period TV series *Mr. Selfridge*, Boe graced the screen, portraying the music hall performer Richard Chapman. The brilliance of Boe's performance did not stop there, as he went on to thrill audiences in two extraordinary ITV Specials, *Ball & Boe: One Night Only* (2016) and *Ball & Boe: Back Together* (2017), alongside the incomparable Michael Ball.

In a turn of events, December 2017 saw Boe stepping into the shoes of the esteemed Aled Jones as the host of ITV's Christmas Carols.

Together with the incomparable Michael Ball, Boe created a musical masterpiece that took the classical music scene by storm. Their collaborative album became one of the best-selling classical albums of the year.

Buoyed by the resounding success of their first album, Boe and Ball embarked on an ambitious follow-up project aptly titled *Together Again.*

In a momentous display of their musical prowess, Boe graced the stage of Ant & Dec's Saturday Night Takeaway on March 3, joining forces with Michael Ball to deliver a show-stopping performance of *The End of the Show* Show.

Boe participated in the thrilling reality competition series, *"Freeze the Fear,"* alongside the renowned Dutch extreme athlete and motivational speaker,

Wim Hof. This British show, hosted by the dynamic duo of Holly Willoughby and Lee Mack, takes contestants on a journey of physical and emotional endurance in subzero conditions.

As part of the show, Wim Hof trains eight celebrities, including Boe, pushing them to their limits through a series of challenging tasks. To provide viewers with an exclusive peek into the behind-the-scenes action, the companion program, *"Munya and Filly Get Chilly,"* offers footage and interviews with the hosts and contestants.

Boe's participation in *"Freeze the Fear"* not only allowed him to showcase his skills but also helped him develop a remarkable ability to maintain composure in front of large audiences. Alongside the incredible Wim Hof, Boe discovered the power of deep breathing, which brought him a sense of ease and control in any situation.

However, Boe's journey to this exhilarating point was not without its struggles. Two years prior to the challenge, he experienced a dark period in his life. The aftermath of his 16-year-long marriage which ended in a divorce left him in a state of deep depression. Seeking solace, Boe turned to drugs, eventually leading him to a five-week stay in a rehabilitation centre.

Yet, as Boe fearlessly plunged into the freezing waters as part of the series' challenge, he experienced an overwhelming sense of relief in his mind and spirit. This moment marked one of the happiest times in his life, as he actively engaged and contributed to the competition.

His eleventh studio album, titled *"As Time Goes By,"* was released the following year by the same label that produced Alfie's previous album. This CD aims to transport listeners to the atmosphere of 1930s New Orleans through its carefully curated selection of music from that era. The tunes exude a relaxed and laid-back vibe, while the piano performance adds a delightful honky-tonk flavour.

Michael Ball and Alfie Boe's collaboration, *'Back Together,'* marked their triumphant return with their third studio album. Since its release by Decca Records in November, this sensational album has soared to the impressive position of number two on the esteemed UK Albums Chart. Garnering predominantly positive reviews, with only a few minor critiques, it has solidified its place as a must-have for music enthusiasts.

As of September 2022, *'Back Together'* had already sold a staggering 214,995 copies in the UK alone. Remarkably, this album marks both Michael Ball's tenth and Alfie Boe's eighth album to crack the illustrious Top Ten in the UK.

Within the captivating melodies of *'Back Together,'* listeners will discover a treasure trove of timeless tracks from the electrifying rendition of *'The Greatest Show'* to the soul-stirring interpretation of *'My Way,'* and the emotionally charged *'Something Inside So Strong.'*

The following year marked the release of the English duo's subsequent studio album, *Together at Christmas.* This album, released by the same record company, soared to the top spot on the prestigious UK Albums Chart upon its initial release. Packed with well-known Christmas songs and an original track titled *"My Christmas Will Be Better Than Yours,"* this CD was a delightful offering amidst the challenges of the Global Pandemic Year.

To further spread holiday cheer, Ball and Boe meticulously planned a 13-show arena tour across the UK in November 2021 to promote this record. As of September 2022, the album impressively sold 160,388 copies in the UK alone.

Their fifth studio album together, aptly titled *Together in Vegas*, showcases a blend of musical styles, including beloved favourites like *"Viva Las Vegas"* and *"Luck Be a Lady."* This album reached an impressive peak position of #3 on the UK Albums Chart, captivating listeners with a total of 51 minutes and 43 seconds of musical brilliance.

In a surprising turn of events, in 2022, Boe did a performance on ITV's *Love Island.* During a secret proposal date, he serenaded Ekin-su and David, leaving an indelible mark on their hearts.

In Boe's World…

After triumphing over countless competitors to secure the lead role in Baz Luhrmann's acclaimed production of Puccini's *La Boheme* in San Francisco back in 2002, Boe's path crossed with that of Sarah, a talented Shakespearean actor, and love blossomed between them. Two years later, they sealed their commitment to marriage, and their family was further enriched with the arrival of their daughter, Grace, and son, Alfred Robert.

During the initial lockdown, the family sought solace within the serene confines of their Cotswolds abode. However, their journey together took an unexpected turn in August 2020, as Boe's professional obligations became a strain on their relationship, ultimately leading to their separation.

In the aftermath of their breakup, Boe wasted no time in listing their shared Cotswold residence for sale, a mere few weeks later. The historic 300-year-old grade II mansion, which was on the market for £2.5 million, boasts an array of luxurious amenities, including an inviting outdoor pool, a state-of-the-art movie theatre, a well-equipped fitness centre, and a pristine tennis court. Additionally, the former home of Alfie offers a meticulously manicured garden and breathtaking vistas of the surrounding countryside. Meanwhile, Boe found himself grappling with the depths of despair following the dissolution of his relationship. Overwhelmed by self-doubt and self-loathing, he spiralled into a dark abyss, resorting to substance abuse that ultimately landed him in a rehabilitation facility for an extensive month-long stay.

On August 24, 2020, Boe revealed that his divorce from Sarah had been very amicable. However, despite the friendly nature of their separation, he still finds himself missing her deeply. The pain of their breakup still feels as fresh as if it had happened just yesterday.

On the other hand, Boe is affiliated with the exclusive Water Rat fraternity. This prestigious group was established in London in 1889 by Joe Elvin and Jack Lotto, both renowned music hall comedians. The Grand Order of Water Rats serves as a fraternal and benevolent institution, primarily focused on supporting individuals working in the entertainment industry.

The fraternity dedicates a significant portion of its resources to aiding hospitals, health charities, and other noble causes. They achieve this by organizing performances and events aimed at generating funds. Membership to this esteemed group is limited to only 180 male industry professionals, with an additional 20 Companion Rats. These distinguished individuals proudly wear a small gold insignia in the shape of a water rat on their lapels.

Throughout the years, the title of the orders' annual King Rat has changed hands numerous times, symbolizing the fraternity's dynamic nature. Additionally, to cater to female performers, including spouses, sisters, and daughters of male performers, a sister organization called the Grand

Order of Lady Ratlings was founded in 1929. The official magazine of the Grand Order of Water Rats is aptly titled The Trap, serving as a platform for members to stay connected and informed.

Boe was awarded an OBE in the 2019 Birthday Honours for his remarkable contributions to music and philanthropy.

This award is considered one of the most prestigious honours bestowed upon British citizens. Established in 1917, this chivalric order recognizes outstanding achievements in the arts, sciences, volunteer service, and public duty. Comprising of five tiers, the highest two bestow the esteemed titles of knight and dame. Appointments to the order are made by the British monarch and senior officers. The order's chapel is located in St. Paul's Cathedral and is accompanied by ceremonial robes and other regalia. However, spouses of Knights and Dames do not receive a title equivalent to Sir or Dame.

The Wild Side

Boe battled alcoholism and rough sleeping on his journey to fame after dropping out of high school. His uncontrollable anger led him to punch a wall, resulting in a broken hand. While he appeared to be living the dream of touring Europe with his group, he was secretly struggling with alcoholism. In 2014, Alfie, a former alcoholic, revealed that he would occasionally abstain from drinking for extended periods, only to fall back into destructive drinking binges. He admitted that alcohol had become his default method of relieving stress.

In pursuit of his passion, Boe left the opera company to enrol at London's prestigious Royal College of Music. His striking appearance caught the attention of numerous attractive female students, earning him a reputation as a Casanova. His actions left Alfie astonished. However, this period was challenging for Boe as he grappled with financial difficulties and uncertainty about his career, which plunged him into deep melancholy.

One night, he ventured into the heart of Soho, making his way to Ronnie Scott's jazz club. Little did he know that this evening would take an unexpected turn. As he embarked on the cab ride back home, a wave of illness washed over him, leaving him incapacitated. The next thing he knew, he found himself sprawled on the floor of his university's common room, awakening to a scene that sent shivers down his spine. The sheer terror of it all left him deeply unsettled.

During his second year, Alfie shared an apartment with three roommates who had a penchant for filling the air with the pungent smoke of their marijuana. Although he occasionally indulged in smoking himself, he understood the importance of safeguarding his voice as a singer. This knowledge compelled him to exercise caution.

Alfie also had a peculiar encounter while performing in Amsterdam. Unbeknownst to him, he consumed hashcakes, which had a lasting impact on his mental state. The ensuing anxiety and paranoia made it challenging for him to evaluate his own performance objectively. Realising that the influence that surrounded him hindered his personal growth, Alfie made the unconventional decision to leave the apartment and take solace on a bench in Hyde Park, ensuring his rucksack was securely fastened to his ankle to deter any potential theft.

Furthermore, there are numerous instances of Alfie's eccentric behaviour, such as his inclination for physical outbursts. Upon learning that his mother disapproved of his affinity for non-classical music, he vented his frustration by forcefully striking his palm against a wall, an act of rage that left him injured. Another time, in a fit of anger, he pounded on a door with such intensity that he inadvertently lost a ring from his finger.

During a performance in Cardiff, Alfie found himself in a rather peculiar situation. As the audience was engrossed in his act, a disruptive ringtone pierced through the air. Without missing a beat, Alfie took matters into his own hands. Seizing the woman's mobile, he deftly pressed the redial button. With the device now positioned near his microphone, he took a moment to address the unexpected interruption. In a calm yet firm tone, he informed the woman's mother that he was currently in the midst of a captivating show.

Currently, Alfie appears to be calmer and more in control of his aggression than the way it was in the past.

The Friendship Bond

Unusual circumstances brought about the friendship between Alfie and Michael Ball. Alfie, a student facing difficulties, happened to be renting a room near Michael Barnes' house. Desperate for guidance,

Alfie slipped a message into the mailbox of the renowned theatre star.

Unfortunately, he received no response.

In 2007, fate intervened and Alfie and Michael found themselves sharing the stage at the London Coliseum for the ill-fated English National Opera production of Kismet. Despite the disastrous performance, they found solace in each other's company and shared laughter. Little did they know, this would mark the beginning of a remarkable and fruitful relationship. Surprisingly, they were the only ones spared from the harsh criticism, and this unexpected turn of events paved the way for their future success.

Their powerful voices and charismatic charm proved to be a winning combination, leading them to collaborate on five albums and achieve international acclaim. It was a journey they could never have anticipated, but their shared talents and undeniable chemistry propelled them to great heights.

Michael Ball is a renowned English performer in the world of musical theatre, known for his exceptional singing abilities and captivating television presentations. He has graced the stage in notable productions such as Les Miserables and The Phantom of the Opera, leaving a lasting impression on audiences. With numerous chart-topping songs and albums under his belt, including a heartfelt rendition of "You'll Never Walk Alone" alongside Captain Tom Moore, Ball has solidified his position as a musical sensation.

Not only has Ball received acclaim for his roles in *Hairspray* and *Sweeney Todd*, but he has also proudly represented the United Kingdom in the prestigious Eurovision Song Contest. His contributions to the realm of musical theatre have been so significant that he was honoured as an Officer of the Order of the British Empire.

When examining the extensive list of relationships that both Ball and Boe have formed throughout their illustrious entertainment careers, it becomes perplexing as to why their collaboration has endured for such a remarkable duration. Ball, with his outgoing and humorous nature, stands in stark contrast to Boe, who prefers a more reserved and introspective approach. Yet, their dynamic has been likened to the legendary on-screen duo of Walter Matthau and Jack Lemmon. Together, they form a formidable verbal tag team, skillfully building upon each other's responses and engaging in a friendly competition to deliver the wittiest and sharpest remarks.

Despite their differences, Ball and Boe have achieved remarkable success as a duo, selling over a million CDs in the UK. Their talent and hard work have earned them two Classic Brit Awards, and they have had the privilege of performing to sold-out arenas on two separate occasions. In a remarkable feat, they even secured the coveted 2016 Christmas No. 1 slot, surpassing renowned acts like Little Mix and The Rolling Stones.

During an interview, the duo expressed their disapproval when asked about any healthy rivalry between them. Their aversion to competition stems not only from their partnership but also from the fact that they genuinely enjoy performing together. They fear that engaging in a rivalry might jeopardize the strong bonds of friendship they have formed.

One of the aspects that Ball and Boe cherish about touring together is the positive momentum and enthusiasm they experience from playing to new audiences every night. It brings them immense joy and fulfilment. Interestingly, Ball finds it amusing that Boe appreciates the culinary delights, particularly the Bisto gravy, more than the glitz and glamour of show business while travelling.

The pair have faced their fair share of mental health challenges. Boe's divorce triggered a deep depression, which became a significant factor in his internal struggle. However, he managed to seek help and eventually entered a treatment centre, where he successfully overcame his addiction. Michael, having experienced his own battles with mental health, found it particularly captivating to witness Alfie's appearance on Wim Hof's BBC1 program, *"Freeze The Fear"* as it resonates deeply with him.

In 1985, Michael was granted the lead role of Marius in the West End premiere of Les Misérables. However, this achievement was accompanied by a bout of severe depression. At the young age of 23, he was struck by glandular fever, rendering him unable to perform for six weeks. As if that wasn't enough, he also suffered a panic episode on stage, which triggered a series of similar episodes. In that moment, he believed his life was over. Filled with despair, he left the program and secluded himself at home for nine long months, convinced that he would never work again. His fear of being in public intensified, leading to an extreme aversion to places and situations that could potentially trigger anxiety or panic, such as crowded areas or open spaces. This anxiety condition persisted, and despite his parents' heartbreak, he refused to discuss his struggles with them or anyone else. He felt too afraid to ask for help, so he stumbled through on his own. Unfortunately, that anxiety still lingers within him though it is not severe.

Michael, now realizing the significance of discussing his experience, regrets not doing so earlier. He endured a nerve-wracking breakdown that shattered his self-confidence and belief in his abilities. It was a distressing event that seemed beyond his control. However, he managed to conquer his fears and summon the courage to perform live on a late-night talk show. Despite expecting a limited audience, he forged ahead and delivered a flawless performance, overcoming his jitters. After this triumph, he felt compelled to seek out someone who believed in him and take measures to prevent a recurrence of such an ordeal.

Enter Cameron Mackintosh, the producer who had cast Michael as Marius in Les Misérables. Recognizing the challenges Michael had faced, Mackintosh offered him the role of Raoul in the revamped production of *The Phantom of the Opera.* In addition to finding support, Michael also sought ways to redirect his attention during moments of anxiety. Inspired by Stephen Gately, the vocalist of Boyzone, he adopted a technique of tapping into the body's energy channels to alleviate panic attacks. Although he still experiences occasional episodes of panic, he now employs this method before performances, finding solace in its effectiveness.

During an interview for his role in *Aspects of Love*, he had a fateful encounter with his future wife, Cathy McGowan, the esteemed host of *Ready Steady Go!* This meeting proved to be a turning point in his life, as he attributes her presence to saving him from the depths of depression and self-destruction. Fast forward eleven years, on the eve of Christmas, tragedy struck as their beloved home was engulfed in flames. In this dire situation, Cathy once again emerged as his saviour.

It was during the festive period.

Before retiring to the guest bedroom, he sought solace in a few sips of whisky and some Night Nurse to alleviate his cold symptoms. Little did he know that fate had other plans for him that night. As Cathy woke up coughing, panic set in. The room was shrouded in darkness, and he was nowhere to be found beside her in bed. Where could he possibly be, she wondered. Frantically searching the house, her efforts to locate him proved futile. Finally, she discovered him and forcefully dragged him out of bed and out of the burning house, before returning to rescue their loyal canine companion.

The fire ravaged their cherished possessions, including precious mementoes, gold discs, films, and DVDs, leaving nothing but ashes in its wake. The cause of this devastating inferno was an electrical failure. Despite the heart-wrenching loss, they find solace in the fact that they escaped with their lives. However, the impact of this traumatic event weighed heavily on Cathy, as haunting dreams continued to plague her while Michael's recollection of that fateful evening remained hazy at best. The severity of Cathy's trauma forced them to make the difficult decision of selling their family home. Somehow, they still live in constant fear and caution, forever scarred by the terrifying ordeal they endured.

Even though they have been together for 33 years without getting married, they have never had children due to a tragic incident that occurred when Michael was 18. Michael's devastating impotence was a result of a burst groin and intestinal haemorrhage. In 1999, he revealed that the severe internal injuries he sustained as a young man during a charity parachute jump left him unable to father children. He recounted being dragged across the ground during the descent, which happened much faster than he had anticipated due to the incident. Even though he doesn't have a child of his own, he has a stepdaughter, Emma and he is the grandfather of her children.

Michael claims the breakdown improved his performance and character, and it applies the same to Alfie.

To raise money for mental health organisations, Alfie plans to continue exposing himself to sub-zero temperatures (*Freeze The Fear*). Alfie is a dedicated advocate for Outward Bound, an organisation that uses wilderness experiences to instil self-confidence in young people. At 16, he enrolled in an Outward Bound programme, which helped him become more open to taking risks. A former apprentice auto mechanic with a strong northern accent, Alfie utilised the training he had received at Outward Bound as a young man to take on the teachers who wouldn't support him.

Despite the loss of their early mentors, both Michael and Alfie have gone on to have successful professions. Michael Ball's father, Tony Ball, was a significant presence in his upbringing as well. Ball spent part of his formative years in South Africa. At the time, Apartheid reached its zenith. They didn't have access to televisions, and there was strict censorship. In the rental home they were staying in, he could only listen to classical music and a few recordings by Ella Fitzgerald, Dean Martin, and Frank Sinatra. This is how he learned to sing on his own. They taught him how to phrase things and how to regulate his breathing. As a young adult, he started going to musicals. At the tender age of 12, Ball was inspired to pursue a career in the theatre after seeing *Jesus Christ Superstar.*

His father took him to the theatre often times, there, he was exposed to Shakespeare. At the time, he was a young theatrical actor who was also failing every class he took. He was completely at a loss as to his future plans. Fortunately for him, a member of the Surrey County Youth Theatre audience approached him and asked whether he had ever considered enrolling in a theatre school. Such thought never ran through his mind but he didn't hesitate to give it a try. Just when he was ordered to leave his private school because he was failing his A-levels, he auditioned for and was accepted into the Guildford School of Acting. Sadly, when he was finally finding his feet in the career world, Michael's adored grandma, Agnes (Lil) wasn't there to celebrate with him.

Notwithstanding the fact that his parents were always there for him, his grandma was his real inspiration. She was a formidable Welsh matriarch in the traditional sense, and her devotion to Ivor Novello served as an inspiration to him. His grandma saw his aptitude and pushed him to play dress-up, which resulted in some hilarious recordings of him and his cousins acting out various superhero and villain roles. His grandmother, Lil, had a big *influence* on him as he prepared for the role of Edna Turnblad in the musical Hairspray. Even though she adored the Welsh vocalist Ivor Novello, she discouraged her grandson from imitating Harry

Secombe. Michael auditioned for a part in the play The Pirates of Penzance after seeing an ad for it in the publication The Stage. His grandma was so ecstatic with his success that she went about proclaiming to anybody who would listen, "That's my boy!" as she showed them the reports and bragged about him in their neighbourhood. But tragically, she died away suddenly only days before she was to see him in the play.

After the performance, he went back to the dressing room to find his mother waiting for him. He had sensed that it was bad news. Just as he had suspected, his mother informed him that his grandma had died. It was so devastating that it led him to depression and self-despair.

Over the years, Ball and Boe have bonded and nurtured their relationship to become not just significant figures in the musical world but best of buddies.

Jenkins and Boe's Rivalry

As part of the alleged feud between Alfie and Katherine Jenkins, Alfie was accused of writing the C-word on a poster of Katherine Jenkins. Katherine and Alfie are two opera-lite singers who once shared the stage during their performance at the London version of *Carousel*. Several sources claim that the two had a chilly relationship, with tensions arising over the size of their respective dressing rooms and the sequence in which they took their final bows. While Jenkins had thought the controversy had ended, someone told her that Alfie had damaged one of her advertising posters with the C-word.

The Sun reports that as Katherine was signing albums at the Manchester HMV, she saw the store's employees desperately attempting to hide a poster. Despite their efforts, she noticed that her poster was ruined with a C-word written on it. When she inquired to know, she was told that Alfie was responsible for it. Meanwhile, Alfie has come out to clear his name and correct the record, claiming that after three years he has "nothing but respect" for the artist.

Facts

- Alfie listens to a lot of The Who, Freddie Mercury, and Queen.

- Alfie enjoys watching films, particularly on extended trips. While travelling, he likes to watch films he's missed. He lists *Easy Rider, National Lampoon's Vacation, The Good, the Bad,* and *the Ugly, Raging Bull,* and *Back to the Future* as his all-time favourite movies. However, he admits that his favourites tend to fluctuate depending on the occasion.

Summary

His musical CDs combine classical music, show songs, and popular music, and he is most renowned for his work in musical theatre. He was born Alfred Giovanni Roncalli Boe in 1973, in Blackpool, UK. Named after Pope John XXII's Italian name, he was the ninth and last kid. When Boe was just 17 years old, a customer at the TVR plant in Bispham who had links in the music industry noticed him singing and recommended he try out for the D'Oyly Carte Opera Company in London. The Royal Opera House, National Opera Studio, and the Royal College of Music in London welcomed him after his successful audition. He landed a starring part in a Broadway production of *"La Boheme"* in 2002, recorded a recording with the company, and shared a Tony Honours Award with his co-stars the following year. *"Classic FM Presents Alfie Boe"* was his first solo album, released in 2006. A movie and record titled *Les Misérables in Concert: The 25th Anniversary* featured him as Jean Valjean. He performed in a variety of staged plays, including *"The Mikando"* by Gilbert and Sullivan and *"Carousel"* by Rodgers and Hammerstein, and also participated in many performances at the *BBC Proms.* For his contributions to music and philanthropy, he was made an Officer of the Order of the British Empire in 2019. He performs classical and popular music performances throughout the United Kingdom and the United States, both as a soloist and in collaboration with other musicians. He was hitched to Sarah Boe from 2004 till they divorced in 2020. Grace and Alfred Robert are their children.

As part of his future events, he will be hosting *Scala Radio Presents: Classics at Christmas* at The London Palladium. The event which is scheduled to be held on Sunday, November 26 at 3 p.m., with feature performances by the Royal Philharmonic Concert Orchestra. Besides the hosting role, Alfie Boe will be performing on stage with additional musicians which will be revealed with time.

Printed in Great Britain
by Amazon

35711912R00051